MESSAGE TO GOD

MESSAGE TO GOD

Franck Olivier Houngnikpo

VILLAGE TALES PUBLISHING
LAWRENCEVILLE, GA

Available from Amazon.com and other retail outlets
ISBN: 9780985362584
LCCN: 2015937164
Available on Kindle and other devices
eISBN: 9780985362591

Printed in the United States of America

DEDICATION

I dedicate this book to my dearest
Miss Angels Roka Bokuakasi,
and to my siblings:
Justice, Félicité, Valerie,
Speed and Ken Houngnikpo.

CONTENTS

ACKNOWLEDGEMENT

Indeed, I thank God Almighty for giving me the strength and courage to write this book, which of course wouldn't have been completed without the expertise and advice of Mr. Augustine Sherman, the financial sponsorship of Mr. François Xavier Adjakidje, and, Emmanuel Aziawa. Much thanks to Herman Mensah, Uriel Agbedja, Marius Ahonon, Patrick Agoli-Agbo; and not forgetting my dear uncle, Mathurin C. Houngnikpo, and my dearest granny, Dansikpe Houngnikpo.

All my gratitude to Mr. Serge Baweyou, Caleb Gbehede, Alain Guedegbe.

I thank Mr. Dan Comlanvi Prosper Jean-Baptiste, Brown Prosper Ozioma, Zacharie Mbaiadoum Ngarabe, Drish Hillman Sendje and Miss Ophelie Folly, and also, Madame Chantal Saizonou for her unconditional support.

And last but not least, my thanks go to everyone in Benin Students and Trainees Association in Ghana (Association des Etudiants et Stagiaires Beninois au Ghana - AESBeG).

INTRODUCTION

Everyone believes in something that is special and unique; a kind of belief that is beyond understanding. It may be God, Allah, Buddha, or gods... whatever you prefer to call it. Even if a person says he doesn't believe in anything at all, he yet believes that he doesn't believe. And that in itself is another belief. At the end of the day, he does believe that he doesn't believe.

As humans, our beliefs are what alter our actions, behaviors, and determine the paths we would eventually follow. Our beliefs make us more or less alive, intense, vivid or dull. From childhood, we've grown to learn the ways and beliefs of our parents and relatives. Their teachings reflected what they believed would comfort us; keep us healthy, good, and well-mannered. Because, we automatically copy everything we were taught during our youth, we often grow up with similar beliefs. But sometimes along the way, we tend to change direction from that belief—In Africa, tradition, culture or customs are usually deeply rooted—because we are now matured and see things differently. As adults, we think and learn on our own, which means our parents no longer decide for us. They may advise, but not impose their ideology on us.

However, should their teachings convince us while we were growing up, when we come adults, we hold on to that conviction if it justifies positive continuity. If not, we quickly alter it into what we now believe is right for us, or what we imagine is the right God to commit our devotion. At this point, we are finally strengthened to go further in whatever ambition we desire to pursue.

Our strengths are acquired from different sources. Known or not, these sources are the basis on which we build our minds. I most certainly believe there is a God, and wholeheartedly believe in him. This then is where I inevitably get my strength. Others believe in Allah, Buddha or Voodoo as sources of their strengths. I, on the other hand, like many others, believe GOD, the creator of heaven and earth is the one true God. And as long as we live, that state of mind will remain our psychological disposition.

Every step we make reminds us about the rules and regulations of the scriptures we are either following, or disobeying. If subjective to the latter, fear or anxiety is generated from recognizing the consequences of violating these established rules or laws of the scriptures. If we kill, cheat, lie or do bad things, we will be punished—a fundamental reason why we shouldn't kill, cheat, lie or do bad things. In other words, if we follow God's laws, life becomes much easier. But by choosing the wrong path, we make life difficult for ourselves. As reasonable beings, we are most certainly aware of our actions. When we behave good or badly, we are quite mindful of their implications.

And now, we pray, praise, chant and glorify to bless whatever we think we believe in—God, Allah, Buddha or Voodoo. Possible or not, we ask for all sorts of things in hope they would give it to us. Faithful to them or not, we cry, we jump… we even kill ourselves for them. But behind it all, the bottom line is, we always seem to be in need of something. And because of this, we send messages to God for him to respond to.

As there are different types of letters, different types of ideas exist. According to our demands, they are called, 'messages.' If we have requests for God, there should be a way to present them. So, the question is, how do we present the messages we send to our God?

After having abortions for many years, a young lady now wants a child—He studied for many years and would like to get a good job after graduation—He isn't happy with his job; therefore, he would like to seek employment elsewhere—He is so lucky, two or more ladies are pursuing him. Which one will he choose?—Before they eat or do anything, they first ask God for His blessing—She is about to travel, but has a question to ask—They fight every day, but really want to stop—We think there is an evil spirit among us, and believe we should fight against it and banish it—He is a thief, and his wish is to never be caught—He doesn't want his lies to be revealed—He is a true believer. He always asks to be more enlightened....

All of the above questions, statements, or concerns could be packaged into messages and addressed to God. At one time or the other, every man has something to ask God. At one time or the other, we all send some kind of message to God. We send these messages because we are happy, sad, promoted, anxious, afraid, exhausted, amazed, sick, curious, demoted, lucky, strong, weak, etc. We put these messages into prayers, or just voice them out. We also write them as I'm going to do, or recite them by heart, which actually means we really don't need to shout at all.

This book is a summary of many types of messages we usually send to God. It is a vade-mecum, or shall I say, 'mini-prayer-dictionary' of all types of our demands. The poor, rich, innocent and guilty, everyone's message is included. Even though we deny Him sometimes, I intend to show how much each of us need God in our lives. At some point, reading these messages will make you choke with laughter. You might find messages that perfectly fit and describe your state of mind. They may capture the way you thought once upon a time, or even think today. Good or bad, it happens to all of us.

This work is a fruit of my imagination. I intend to offend no one. Any names or association, therefore, is strictly coincidental.

CHAPTER ONE

Omniscient God, never stop listening to us

Message One

Just before breaking into their victim's home, a group of armed robbers decided to pray. Their leader led the prayer:

"Almighty God, we are your children. And, whenever a child needs help he runs to his father. He calls on him every time he needs him.

"Each person has his occupation; a job he does best. And arm robbery is what we have chosen to do. Yes, Lord, we haven't been able to succeed in other professions. But in the stealing business, we've been very successful. And because of that, I thank you for making our dreams come true.

"People never stop criticizing us, but every single day we try to get better at what we do. While most people are against us, we know that you are with us. These people we are stealing from are politi-

cians, who are thieves themselves. So you see, Lord, we are really not doing anything bad. They steal moneys that belong to the country. They steal everything they can get their hands on. It is our money, our sufferings, and our sweat, Lord. Therefore, they are the real thieves.

"Oh Heavenly Father, now that we are about to attack the Mayor's house, please clear the way for us. Make sure we are not caught. As usual, help us to succeed in this operation. Not even the police should be alerted about this, Father. Woe unto anyone that comes our way. I'm talking about the Mayor's many security guards. With you on our side, we would crush them. We would crush whoever stands in our path.

"Almighty God, with you, all things are possible, even for those who don't believe in you. We believe in you, God. We've planned to succeed with this operation tonight, but first, we are asking for your blessings. We cherish you; we adore you, Lord, and glorify your name. Besides the mayor's security guards, who obviously would stand on our way during this operation, we really wish to kill no one.

"In your Almighty Name, this is our prayer. Amen!"

I was passing by that night when I overheard the gang of thieves praying. Of course, I froze and didn't move for fear of being shot. Thank God they didn't see me.

At last, I quietly slipped away, running as fast as I could to my friend, Kofi, to tell him what I had witnessed.

Message Two

After studying a whole year for his final exam, Kofi decided to call on God, the Almighty, to bless him with success during his examination. He knelt down and started talking to God:

"In the Name of the Father, the Son and the Holy Spirit, Amen.

"Jesus Christ, come and save me. I know you are my Savior. I cry for your help and intervention. I know all grace belongs to you. Come and save me, Lord. This is the day I have waited for. I've waited a year to sit for this examination. You know how much I need to pass these exams. You know my heart and spirit, Jesus. I haven't consciously harmed anyone. My dad will skin me alive if I don't succeed. I've done my best by learning hard, God, and this is the time for my reward. I need my reward today, Jesus.

"As we start the exam tomorrow, I ask for courage, comprehension, clear-sightedness and precision. I don't want to make silly mistakes. I kneel before you this night, Father, worshiping you as I always do.

"Regarding the subjects I will be tested on tomorrow, give me the spirit of understanding. Save me from humiliation and failure. Let the questions be easy for me, and conveniently to my understanding so that I will get the best grades.

"Jesus, protect me from any evil and hindrance. Send your angels to protect and guide me, Lord. And I will have more reasons to pray and worship you. You've done so much in my life; I don't think this is going to be more than you can handle.

"Once again, guide and protect me, Jesus Christ, in the name of the Father, the Son and Holy Spirit. Amen!"

I waited in silence for him to finish praying. Then when he opened his eyes, he was most astonished to see me standing there that night. I explained my intrusion and he understood.

I spent the night with him, but didn't tell him anything about the thieves.

෴

The following day, I heard that one of my cousins was ill. I hurried to the hospital where he had been admitted.

Message Three

A twenty-one year old man was taken to the emergency room. On hearing the news, the young man's mother ran to the hospital where she learned her son's condition was critical. Doctors were presently working on him, so she wasn't allowed to see him at that moment. She resigned and quietly returned to the waiting room where she tearfully started to pray:

"Oh Lord, I know that I'm a sinner, but have mercy on me. Your word declares that he who knocks; it shall be open to him (Matthew 7:7). Here, I've come to bang on your door. Please, Lord, listen to my prayer. Almighty God, it is my son... that boy is my only son. He is my hope, my future... my everything.

"Oh Jesus Christ of Nazareth, if it is any crime I've committed, may it befall on me, God. Nevertheless, if he'd committed any sin, I wish to bear all his punishments. It is too much for him to carry. The doctors said he has a tumor.

"My son is suffering, Lord, save him. It might be impossible for man, but not for you, Almighty God. Break his chain of pain and suffering, Lord. I believe in you, and I surrender all to you this very moment. I need you to do a miracle in my life, God. I can't stand seeing my son on that bed in agony. Please, Father, who art in heaven, do something for my son.

"In the Almighty Name of Jesus Christ, I pray. Amen!"

And then I responded, "Amen," bringing her to realize I was standing there. She turned, saw me, and burst into tears as she tried to explain my cousin's condition. I couldn't stand her grief, and started to cry too.

࿐

I went home after I left the hospital. As I entered the house, I heard my sister praying joyfully in her room.

Message Four

This is pretty much the prayer of a woman in love with her fiancé. She is certainly not ready to lose him to anything in this world:

"Lord, my God, thank you for giving me such a wonderful man which I jealously intend to keep. Because I understand no one is perfect, each time he steps out without me, I implore you, God; watch over him. May all the women that look upon him with admiration and love go blind. Slap any woman with your invisible hand, God, who imagines and intends to hug and kiss him. If a woman tries to

sit on his lap, may she instantly get diarrhea. Oh Father, Lord, please make sure these females who attempt to lure money from him be consumed by the fire of the Holy Spirit.

"Almighty God, this favor I sincerely ask from you. Nowadays, ladies are very terrible as I was once like them. So, if a woman attempts to book a hotel with the intention of dragging my man into it, she must immediately get her menstruation, accompanied by a violent stomachache. Those who plan to send anonymous SMS to my man, in order to reveal my past, should never get network available.

"I am damn serious, my Lord, please help me. In your name I pray. Amen!"

I thought her prayer was pretty funny and couldn't help my laughter. My sister opened her room door, saw me standing there and screamed wildly. She shoved me, and I tumbled. I found my balance, then told her about our cousin, and she was touched as well. She immediately started out the door for the hospital. I followed her.

On our way, we met one of my sister's friends who joined us. As we continued to the hospital, she explained to us about her prayer to God on the same issue of having met a man.

Message Five

One day, a young lady met a man she didn't know from anywhere. To her surprise, he proposed marriage to her. She didn't know what to say or do, and decided to pray:

"Alleluia! May the Lord be praised! I believe I've just found mine. Thank you, Lord, for this gift.

Perhaps, I'm putting the cart before the horse, but it must be out of love. I barely know this man, Prosper, but I believe I like him. He doesn't have what it takes to go out with me, but he certainly has the main criterion—MONEY. If I should marry him, at least I won't suffer from poverty.

"So, I've come before you, God. I really want to marry Prosper. But there's one important thing... I pray that nothing, absolutely nothing, changes his financial prosperity. I most surely don't want to live in poverty. If his financial situation changes, I would definitely ask for a divorce.

"Furthermore, I pray to you, Almighty God, to open his parents' hearts so that they accept me unconditionally. But, if they don't and try to stand in my way, I won't hesitate to make them pay. Prosper is mine. Usually, I don't like short men, but the fact he has money, I'm prepared to make an exception to that rule.

[Oh, by the way, God, help me to love him as he deserves.]

"And, as I'm here praying to you today, I shall do it again and again, if only you'd help me capture this man. I would definitely be grateful to you. In fact, I shall devote my entire life to serving you.

"Thank you, Jesus, for the door of wealth you have opened for me. It is true that patience is a treasure. I was jumping from one man to another; they were not serious and I wasn't either. I didn't want to indulge any fake marriage. That's the reason why I wasn't serious. Imagine, Oh Lord, if I had tied myself down in any of those previous relations. Today, I wouldn't have hit the jackpot.

[By the way, thank you, Lord, for helping me through my abortion... after that good-for-nothing man put me in the family way.]

*"This is my prayer in your name, as I say,
Prosper is my man. Amen!"*

After listening to my sister's friend, I wondered if I could ever get married. Women are not serious, I thought; then I thought about men and realized women aren't bad after all.

࿊

One day, at my friend's elder brother's wedding, I discovered something terrible. I overheard the newly married groom whispering a monologue in the garden.

<u>*Message Six*</u>

Mark had just gotten married to Anna; that same day he cheated on his wife. Knowing it was a bad thing he had done, and feeling guilty about it, he prayed to God:

"Oh Lord, Jesus, forgive me, for I have sinned. What I've just done is a sin against you, my God. I know it is one of the greatest sins: cheating… adultery… and, I'm sincerely sorry. Please forgive me.

"We are not sinners because we sin, Oh Lord, but we sin because we are all sinners. I have come before you, God, to confess and ask for forgiveness. No one saw me, but you did. I don't want to lose my wife, Anna. She loves me very much, my Lord, and I love her too. What happened was a mistake. Anna should never know anything about it.

"Jesus of Nazareth, when things like this happen, we, men always blame Satan. This, however, is not the case. Oh merciful God, I take responsibility for

my deeds. I promise you and my conscience alone that it will never happen again. When I think about it, I feel sick. How could I cheat on my wife just after our wedding? Oh my God!

"But then, the temptation was irresistible, Lord. She came into the bathroom to me—so provocative, seductive, her bubbling chest bouncing like balloons. Look at her, Lord! Just look at her! I fell into her trap. I guess any man would have. She lured me into it. I wouldn't be lying if I said she was the devil in disguise.

"However briefly, it was sweet, Oh Lord. So, help me never to fall into traps like that again. Somehow, I know the devil is at work. I also know he cannot do anything to this child of God. Please protect me, be my refuge and help me fight against the angels of darkness. They will never succeed in breaking my marriage, NEVER!

"Finally, help me, Oh Lord, to face my wife without shame or suspicion on my face. She shouldn't know about this. In your Powerful Name I pray. Amen!"

On hearing my friend's brother's prayer, I was shocked. I took French leave that day.

ॐ∘ॐ

Because I didn't feel like going home, I went
to one of my friends' workshop instead. He
is a painter.

Message Seven

Due to certain circumstances, the painter and I became friends. Visiting him one day at his workshop,

I discovered something interesting he had written on a painted board. It was placed at the entrance to the workshop. He said it was more like a motto for him, and he read it every day when he arrived at work. It stated:

> "Yes, Lord, I believe you're right. You are Almighty, and your Word is powerful. He who clings onto you will never be disappointed. Every day I knock at your door, asking with prayers and praises, yet my business is still not doing well. Everybody is laughing at me. Why?
>
> "You said we should be faithful to you, ask and pray sincerely, which I always do. But, I never get any answer. I know that I need to be patient, but time waits for no man. I'm getting old, my God.
>
> "Listen, Dear God, you promised me my daily bread. I want it now. Amen."

The last sentence amused me a lot, and I smiled. Otherwise, I was still in a state of shock from listening to my friend's elder brother's prayer. I told the painter what I'd overheard and he felt really sorry for the bride.

❧

The following morning my father sent me
to Labidi, the carpenter. He was also my
friend.

Message Eight

Labidi's carpenter shop was located at the corner, down the street from my house. He did very good work and people appreciated it. But at the time, business had slowed down. I found him on his knees praying for his business. He didn't realize I was there:

"...and you are the Alpha and Omega. Nothing can be done without you. I've come this morning to ask for your pardon. My business is going down and I need to save it. Everything is collapsing around me and I feel pretty bad about it. I need you to help me save it, Lord. Working with wood is what I do best and you know that. I'm a carpenter, one of the best in this town. I make coffins, beautiful coffins... all sizes. Designing sarcophaguses is my specialty.

"My Heavenly God, you know very well what is happening. People are not dying as they used to. They are living longer than before. And that's affecting my business a lot. If people don't die, how will I make money from my profession? How can I live?

If nothing is immediately done about this soon, I will die from hunger, my God. Apart from you, Lord, you know I have no one to help me. I pray this morning that customers rush in to buy my coffins. I would be very glad to sell three to five coffins every day. Yes, help me, Lord.

"For that and more, I pray. Amen."

After listening to his prayer, I had goose bumps. Somehow, I understood his prayer. At last I delivered my message to him and left.

෨෧

On my way back home, I found a purse.
There was a message inside.

Message Nine
A thirty-five year old woman without a child, or

husband, needs to pray hard. She is Miss Frida. In spite of her age, she was still single and prayed every day:

"I thank you, Father God, for waking me up today. Oh how time quickly goes by. I ask myself what I've actually been able to achieve in life. I seem to have no answer.

"When I was eighteen years old, all I ever prayed for was having a handsome man. Back then, I didn't know much about life. I was still dreaming and living in the wonders of fantasies. I thought of the wonderful stories about princes and princesses, Romeo and Juliet… And so, I dreamed about having a handsome man who would come and sweep me off my feet and take me far away to wonderland. I was mistaken.

"When I was about twenty-two, I came back to you, Lord. That time around, I asked you for a rich guy and you gave him to me. By then, I thought I've learned much about life. Little did I know that life is nothing but deep mysteries. I'm discovering that the more we know, the more we realize we know nothing. Oh God, rich men are crazy. I suffered hell with the last one.

"At twenty-six years old, my prayer was to get married. But it was difficult to find a man who was ready to get into a serious relationship. I met all types, but I haven't been satisfied. So, Jesus, my Savior, I've come to you once again. Give me the last chance, my Lord. I'm thirty-five years old now and still childless. God, I know you always listen to my prayers, come to my rescue.

"Almighty God, I plead that you give me a husband. I don't care if he's handsome or rich. And if he doesn't want to get married; just let him get me pregnant. I care less if he's a criminal. I swear

to you, God, I won't abort this time. I shall keep my pregnancy and give birth. Yes, Lord, I need a child. I want to have one. Please listen to me, Dear God.

"In the Name of the Father, the Son, and the Holy Spirit, I pray. Amen."

After reading the message, I realized how desperate some women get in want of a child.

☙

Oh, I just remembered. My mother once
told me about a male student addressing a
message to God.

Message Ten

There are different types of students; they each go to school for different reasons. Jackson is one of those students, and his primary reason for being in school is to chase the ladies. He cares less about learning or paying attention to his teachers. But when the time for examination approaches, he starts complaining and naturally, turns to God:

"Jesus Christ of Nazareth, I know you can hear me. I've come before you this evening to make a deal with you. Please, Lord, the examination is fast approaching and I haven't got any work done yet. I'm studying very hard, but nothing is staying in my mind.

You know how many lessons I have to prepare for this term, God. Help me to focus on those questions that will come during the exam. It's too late to learn all of them. It's too much for me, Lord.

"Please, my God, the exam should be very easy

and understandable, so I can at least get the average mark. Make the person marking my papers to mess up and give me very good marks. Or, let that person alter my marks with those of someone else.

My parents are suffering to send me to school, and I don't want to disappoint them. I don't want to fail and repeat the class, Jesus. Send your angels to enlighten me by whispering the answers into my ears. Lord, give me the chance to cheat without anyone seeing me. Help me, Lord; help me no matter what.

"I pray in the Name of Almighty God. Amen."

Ridiculous, isn't it?

CHAPTER TWO

What if the end were the beginning

Message Eleven

Here we go again. My mother has just called us for dinner. As usual, before eating, she talks to God. Most people pray before eating, drinking, and so does Mama Angels:

> *"Heavenly Father, I praise you and glorify your name because there is nobody like you. You are the beginning... the first and the last. I thank you, Oh Lord, for your blessings, your love and protection. Thank you for providing our daily bread. For those who have nothing to eat, please Lord, provide it for them. Thank you Lord. I know I'm not better than them, but you did it for me. So, please do the same for them.*
>
> *"Oh Father God, please accept my prayer in the name of your Beloved Son whom you sent to deliver us from sins. Amen."*

Thank God her prayer was short this time. My mother usually prays for five or more minutes before we start eating.

∂∘⌒

Then I went to church. As I entered, the
pastor was praying.

<u>Message Twelve</u>

The pastor of our church had gathered his faithful to pray with them. They called it, Intercession Prayer. For me, it was a message to God:

"In the powerful Name of Jesus, I pray. Oh Lord, this is your temple, here are your people. Come among us right this minute, Father Lord. Come and make our lives temples of the Holy Spirit, we pray to you.

"Please, Lord, help us live good lives, give each of us the Fruits of the Spirit: Love, Joy, Peace, Patience, Goodness, Faithfulness, we pray. For we know that you are the beginning and the end. The Holy Scripture is our way, and the Holy Ghost is the power, the flame of God. As we are gathered here tonight, send your Spirit of consolation upon us, Father. Let it shine over those who are in distress. And may your Spirit of Consolation shine over those who are victims of injustice, we pray. Preserve us from hatred and all the countries from war, we pray. Gather the nations around your Holy Fire, Lord, we pray.

"May everybody shout, Amen!"

"Amen!"

It was a powerful message that I fancied so much.
It was brief and consistent.

༺∽༻

I spent that night at Aunt Clariss house.
Early the following morning, just before
leaving, I heard her words.

Message Thirteen

Mrs. Clariss' daily prayer before going to work:

"Father, every morning when I wake up, I thank you. I'm nobody without you. That is why I'm asking you to guide me to live by your laws, full of love, happiness, justice and forgiveness. Help me, Lord, to know your only Son, Jesus Christ, and walk in his footsteps for your kingdom on earth. Let your Word be known and revealed to me. Your Word is a treasure, and I never walk in this wild world without my Holy Bible. Anytime I read your Word, I observe how much I feel good. It vitalizes me and gives me more strength.

"Now that it is day and the sun is shining, I ask you, Oh Lord, to protect me as I walk out of this door. Show me the way, God. Show me your way.

"In Jesus name I pray. Amen."

After she left, I knelt down and did the same thing.
It was my first time talking to God.

༺∽༻

By the way, before I forget, I have a meeting
to attend. See you soon.

Message Fourteen

After the meeting, one of the leaders sent a message to God:

"Thank you, Lord Jesus, for this wonderful moment together with my family and friends. I said before we started that I would give you all the glory if we concluded this meeting peacefully, and with mutual understanding. I plead with you to watch over everyone that has come here today. Although they may have had other things to do, they left them to attend this meeting. Please lead them to their various houses safely, because they deserve it. For those who were unable to attend this meeting, bless them too. Whatsoever they are doing shall prosper, God. Thank you, for I know that you are still, and will always be, the same unchangeable God.

"Let the issue we've discussed come to life. Let us find the way to achieve everything we've said and decided here, dear God. Glory be to God in the highest."

"Amen."

I got to the meeting very late, but thank God I was present for the closing prayer.

৵৽

Did I tell you I followed my sister to the market one day, and found a seller kneeling next to her products praying?

Message Fifteen

This market seller sends a message:

*"Oh Father God, this is another day. As I have
come with joy to sell my goods, I pray you add more
smile and laughter on my face. It is clear to me that
you haven't forgotten me. But I need to remind
you of our deal. This is a market day and I intend
to increase my sales. Father, please send many clients to me today. People I know, and those I don't
know, should come to buy from me today. Let all my
products be sold, in the Almighty Name of our Lord.*

*"Very soon school will resume, and I would have
to pay my children fees. I'm both their Father and
Mother. Please have mercy on me, Lord, and make
this market day my best day ever.*

"In Jesus' Name, your only Son, I pray. Amen."

Opening her eyes, the seller was somehow shy to
learn we were listening and observing her.

৵৵

When I left the market, I went directly
to the church, where I met a certain guy
crying and praying. I listened to him sadly.
He was in quite a bad shape, I should say.

Message Sixteen

When we struggle hard and nothing positive
results from it, we become desperate and sad. Robert
went through such a thing, and this is the message he
sent to God:

*"Why? Oh, why God? What have I done? Why
me? Just tell me what I have done to deserve this.
What sin have I committed to pass through this suffering? Oh Eternal God, how long will I live and*

*anguish in pain? I have nobody but you, God. You
are my Savior, and you are my Shepherd. I endure, I
pray, I sing, I cry, I listen, I scream, but things still
remain the same. It's like my tears are not reaching
the profound side of your heart. It seems my prayers
are not well enough to be taken into account. Please,
if that is the case, show me the best way to do it, my
God. I'm dying of desperation, depression. Heavenly
Father, while I expect my situation to get better each
day that passes by, things get harder. When will all
this hardship end?*

"*Please, Lord, listen to the outcry of your child.
Come and be my upholder, Father Lord. I want
nothing but a push from you, my God. I know that
whenever you stand, no one else can boast. And
when you rise, all heads bow before you. You are
the highest, the most powerful, Lord. Don't let me
be a victim of Satan.*

"*Have the Holy Spirit touched my soul, Lord,
so that I may be transformed and become another
person. Help me surprise all those who are laughing
today. Let me be a real living testimony for you and
your kingdom, Father God. Because I would never
give up on you, here I am with tears once again,
God. I started serving you and so shall it be forever.
I will only have one God... YOU.*

"*Do something new in my life, Father; something new and awesome. I pray that any evil spirit
surrounding me, burns in your consuming fire.
Break, Oh Father, Lord, all the chains that are pre-
venting me from doing anything good out of my life.
I pray today that your light brightens my life and
give it a new direction.*

"*In your beloved Jesus' name I pray. Amen.*"

Tears effortlessly raced down my cheeks. I felt my

heart beat as if I was in his shoes. Without saying a word, I quietly left.

ᔰᔲ

While watching a film one day, I was privileged to get a message from it. Let me tell you about it.

Message Seventeen

A seven year old little boy sends a message to God:

"In the Name of the Father, the Son and the Holy Spirit, I pray.

"God, are you there? Can you hear me? Well, I know you can hear me and even see me.

"I just have a little favor to ask you, my God. I'm only a child and don't have money to offer you as my father does every Sunday in church. But, I guess that doesn't prevent me from asking. My father said that you listen to everybody and anybody, no matter who.

"Your heart is so broad and pure that you never see any stain or dirt on anyone. So, please watch over my mom. You've called her and she is now with you in heaven. Please, take good care of her as my father always did. My mother was a good woman, and I love her so much. Also, tell her that I love her very much. Tell her that dad loves her as well. We all do. But now that she is no more, I pray that you never let her get married to another man. Because, when you call my dad and me, we shall come there to join her in heaven with you, and we shall be a family again.

"That is the least thing I wanted from you,

Lord. Thank you for listening to my prayer. In the Name of the Father, the Son and the Holy Spirit, I pray. Amen."

Yes, how touching! As far as I'm concerned, that boy has the most innocent way of talking to God.

৵৽ঌ

I'm no genius, but I'm a very good student. So, on this particular day, I went to help one of my classmates with mathematics. Something strange happened.

Message Eighteen

Bertha and her friend, Vanessa, were studying together when the light suddenly went out. Everywhere became dark and Bertha started to pray.

"Blood of Jesus! Satan, you are a liar! Evil angels, you are all defeated in the Name of Jesus. Whatever plan you have made against us this evening shall never succeed. I pray in the Name of the Almighty God that you, evil spirits are all banned in this house.

"Lord, we are protected by the blood of Jesus Christ of Nazareth. As God is in control, no harm can reach us. This instant, we are praying against any demonic spirit present in here. Let the light of God surround us. Let the power of God protect us, and the presence of God watches over us. I command you by the power of God, and the incarnation of Jesus Christ to move out of this place immediately.

"In the Name of God the Father, the Son and the Holy Ghost, I pray. Amen."

She prayed with passion and anxiety. But little did she know that it was the prepaid card which had simply run out. There weren't any Satan or evil spirits in the house. When her mate told her the card had run out, she felt embarrassed.

৯৯৯

A friend of mine was about to travel, and the following is his message.

Message Nineteen

Benjamin is about to travel. He knelt down, closed his eyes and started praying:

"In the Powerful Name of God, I am going on this journey. May God the Father be with me, may the Son protect me, and may the Holy Ghost be by my side. I give you all glory and adoration. Blessed is my protection when I am on my way going. Oh Father Lord, give your angels control to guide me and lead my path so that no wild beast tears me into pieces.

"I thank you, Lord, for always being with me and watching over me. Let me go safely and return safely. No witchcraft or enchantment can harm me. Spare me, Oh God, from road accidents or plane crashes. Bless me, Lord, that I may complete my journey safely and successfully, under your ever watchful care. Amen."

Indeed, anything can happen at any time. He was right. But what about that woman or man who is going to war?

༁

James is getting ready to go abroad on
another military mission.

Message Twenty

James is a brave soldier. He went to many battles
and won. He is getting ready to go on another mission
abroad. He is going to fight and shoot. He has a message for God:

*"I never went to battle, Lord, without your
permission. The time has come again, when we are
sent to another country to fight and shoot to kill one
another. Almighty God, let my fate be strong, let my
courage be bolted and never faltered. Oh Father God,
help me to have enough strength to face the enemies.
Eternal Lord, let our leaders and masters have the
right information and help us in their decisions.
This is a deadly mission, Lord—kill or be killed.*

*"Heavenly Father, if anyone gets in my way,
help me kill that person instantly and be saved.*

*"I've come before you, Lord, to ask for protec-
tion. I ask for courage to face and overcome my fears.
Give me the blessings to get where no one has ever
been able to reach. Accompany me as I go, and be
with me until I return, God. This fight deserves a
great reward, Papa God. And, whenever I receive a
reward, it is in your Holy Name.*

"In your Son's name, I pray. Amen."

When I asked him why he had prayed, he said that
he couldn't make it alone.

CHAPTER THREE

Deep inside our heart, we believe

Message Twenty-One

Travelling is discovering. Every time I travel, I discover something new. I often travel to my uncle for vacation. Whenever I'm there, I notice that he frequently talks to God about his family's welfare; something my father never does. I mean, I've never seen him doing it.

A good father always prays for the welfare of his family:

"In the Name of the Lord Jesus Christ, strengthened by the intercession of the immaculate Virgin Mary, I pray today for my entire household. I know there is no better guard like you. Please, Lord, watch over my family, a family that is so dear to me. I need a powerful intervention, God, to guide them... my wife, my children, as well as my relatives.

"I call upon the power and protection of the Blood of our Lord Jesus Christ over my life. Heav-

enly Father, let no harm or threat get closer to my beloved. I will fear no evil, because you are with me. Help us to always be together so that the enemy never gets a chance to come among us. Send your angels of peace, let them watch over us, God, and keep us protected; body and soul. We belong to your family, Father God, and no one else.
     "In the Name of Jesus Christ, our Lord, I pray. Amen."

I was very touched to hear that we are all he has, and we were important to him.

≈∽∾

When a man is undermined in the society,
he becomes a public phenomenon.

<u>*Message Twenty-Two*</u>

You wouldn't dare force me to tell you the name of the company, would you? Anyway, it is a well known company here in town, where Mr. Tago works. He has worked there for the last seven years. The only odd thing is that his position in the company hasn't changed. A new promotion is coming up this year so Mr. Tago sends this message to the Lord:

"For seven good years now, I've worked for this company. Yet, I've never been promoted. Though they say I'm respectful and a good worker, I don't exactly know why my salary has not increased up to now. This time around, I'm going to fight for my rights, and you are going to help me, God.
     "I've suffered a lot for this company, and it's time it pays me back. This coming promotion has to

be mine. I'm the one they should promote this time. I swear to you, Lord, I'll do all in my power to get my new position. I'll never disgrace you, Father Lord. But if they are not willing to give me the position in peace; please, Lord, show me the way. Show me the shrine of the best spiritualist in this country, and I'll force them to give it to me. I believe they won't be able to resist that one.

"In your Greatest Name I pray. Amen."

God's way is the best, but it needs time. It will be difficult for the one who is impatient to follow God.

❧

I asked one of my wayward friends to take me to where prostitutes hangout. I wanted to see if what people say about them is actually true.

Message Twenty-Three

Standing alongside the road, a prostitute exhibited that familiar expression, consistent with luring clients. Sex has become a game, and these women simply use their bodies—God's precious gifts—as toys to be played with. Now in a whisper, this prostitute sends a message to God:

"Fine, Lord, send me clients. More than twenty men have just passed by and none has stopped to proposition me. I can't believe anyone wouldn't like to sleep with me. Every one of them passed right by and went to the other girls. What do they have that I don't?

"Father God, I was once the choice of all the

rich men in this town. But what is happening to me now? Since these fresh, young girls joined us in this business, I've lost most of my clients.

"My Father Lord, please, I want to still sell my body a little longer before retiring. Look at my shape; it's not what it used to be. My beauty is quickly fading. But Lord, as you well know, I still have the energy to satisfy men....

"One of them is coming this way. Lead him straight to me, Lord Jesus. Let me show him that I'm a sex machine... Damn! He's stopping—that young girl again... no, he's still coming. Good Father, please, please, please... He's stopping again. Isn't he coming to me, God? Oh my God! He's looking at me. Let me look a little sexier... that's it. Yes. He's coming. He's approaching. Yes, Lord, you're definitely doing your job. Oh, God, make sure he accepts me, please...?"

The man stopped directly in front of her and said something to her. She seemed pleased, as she slipped her arm through his, then they walked away together.

Something told me she should have ended her prayer with a,

"Yes, Lord, you are great! Thank you so much. If it hadn't been for you, I wouldn't have gotten this guy. I'm sincerely grateful, my God. Amen."

In response to it all, without realizing it, tears had settled in my eyes. My friend just stood there, observing me with laughter. But, for me, it wasn't funny. The entire unfolding drama was rather sad. Sometimes I wonder how we get to a certain point in our life.

Message Twenty-Four

A man from nowhere, living in abject poverty, asked himself how come he ended up in his current prosperous state. He never understood how it all happened. He had so many questions to ask and never knew how or where to begin. Then, he decided to transform his questions into a message to God:

"Dear God, how come I was an abject nobody and now you've made me somebody? I had nothing, and now, I have everything a man could possibly want. I was lonely, with no friends and no one to talk to; but now, I have many friends. No one honored me, and now I'm overwhelmed with merits.

"You have changed me. You made me a man. You took a part of me and made of it a family. Now, I have a home and a family. Why wouldn't I praise you, Oh Lord? I know you are the Almighty, the beginning and the end. But I still want to know more about your powers.

"Show me, Oh Lord, your mercy and love that never gives up. I have many reasons to praise and glorify your name. But in order to understand your power, I still want to know the magic. I will keep on waiting. Don't be long because I'm not getting any younger.

"Through Jesus Christ, your Beloved Son, I pray. Amen."

If this ever happens to you, you would understand what that man meant.

∞∞

I once had a dream about a lady who received bad news. She prayed all night.

Message Twenty-Five

A certain lady studying abroad had just received bad news. Her dear and beloved mother was sick. Naturally, she became stressful and confused. This is part of the message she sent to God:

"For your love and mercy, I know that nothing bad will happen to my mother. God of all nations, please help my mother recover as soon as possible. She is my mother and I love her so much. It is no doubt that you love her too, because she is also your daughter.

"Here I am, far away from my family. Apart from you, God, my mother is all I have in this world. I look to you to watch over her and save her from whatever disease it is. Please, Oh Lord, provide her the necessary help she needs. I know there is no better doctor than you. You are our savior, and I pray in the Name of your Beloved Son to treat her. I count on you to cast out any illness that is disturbing her life. Her life belongs to no sickness, no evil; but only to YOU, God.

"Yes, Father, you know I would soon complete my studies. You can understand how much I still need her, God. She's the only one that pays my school fees. So, please, God of mercy, do something right now and let me hear better news. I can't wait.

"Amen, in your Holy Name."

Although devastated about the news of her mother's sickness, she was also concern for her own interest. Nothing goes for nothing.

ॐ

Do you think the fetishist also needs God?

Message Twenty-Six

A fetishist always consults his gods when there is a problem. He first listens to his visitors, then turns to his gods. He explains everything to the gods and listens to them in return. If there was anything at all to do, he readied himself for it. He would praise, pray and chant to his gods. He would tell them what is expected from them. Above all, the fetishist would send a quick message to the highest God, the Creator of heaven and earth:

> *"... And I bow to the Highest God. I've come to you because I know you are the Almighty. I put the life of these people into your hands. I, also hereby, present their problems to you so that you can take control. In the Name of the Highest God, I pray...."*

Even if the fetishist isn't vocal, yet he prays to God in his heart.

> *"...Forgive me, Lord, for not praying loudly. But I know that you are the Most Powerful. Whatever I do here would never function if you do not accept. Please, Lord, accept my prayer so that these people would get the results of their wishes. In your Mighty Name, I pray. Amen."*

Don't be chocked with laughter, but above anything, the fetishists do pray to God. They just feel too proud sometimes to spill it out loudly.

～◌～

Siana is my niece. She was born a week ago, and everyone is so contented to have her.

Message Twenty-Seven

She is a new born baby called, Siana. Her father and mother are overjoyed with their infant daughter. Relatives and visitors come from all around, one after another, to visit little Siana and wish her well. This is a message from one of the visitors:

"Father God, Creator of all beings and the entire universe, we've come before you. We bless your name and praise you and your wonders, the work of your hand and your infinite wisdom. Thank you, Lord, for the time and patience you've taken to create this little baby. You have given her the beauty of nature. We are all proud of you, Lord. We thank you for the power and qualities you have given to this child so that she could, in the near future, be unique and special for her kind.

"Please God, help her parents teach her the path of good manners in life. Let them guide her through your light and according to your will. Let this new-born baby bring joy and pride to her parents.

Oh Father Lord, you so love this world that you sent your only Son to come and die for our sins. Make sure that your love and affection flow in this baby's veins. This place is a wild world where we fight, and fight restlessly.

"Father God, send your angels to guard this child against all evil forces. Give the necessary strength to her parents to protect her. May she never lose in life, but always win.

Almighty God, bless her with people that will sincerely protect and guide her along life's path. Open great opportunities and favorable doors for this innocent child. Our prayer is to see her at the top and as a winner one day in the future. We pray for success and progress in her life.

"In the Name of your Beloved Son, we pray. Amen."

Welcome to the new world, my dearest niece.

❧❦

And now, how would you feel if you are accused wrongly? I've heard the message of a man who was a victim of injustice.

Message Twenty-Eight

A man has been accused of a crime he didn't commit. "Guilty," they said. He sent a quick message to God:

"Almighty God, on my judgment day, I know you'd be the only true judge. Today, they have found me guilty. I accept. But you know I'm not guilty, Father God. I tried many times to explain my side of the story, but they just wouldn't listen. I guess this is the same way they accused your only Son, Jesus Christ. They made him suffer, and then killed him.

"Oh Father, have mercy on them for they don't know what they are doing. What has happened was a sheer coincidence. I didn't kill that man. Yes, he slept with my woman, nevertheless, I never thought of killing him.

"My enemies take pleasure to have succeeded, but I reject it in the Name of Jesus Christ. They think I'm condemned, but I know soon I would be delivered by the Power of God. To them, my life is no longer worthy. But on the contrary, my life has just taken a new turn.

"Father, I bring to you each person who is

oppressed just like me, who is treated unjustly or overlooked unfairly. Please, Lord, help them out. We have no one but you, God. Father, take each of these persons into your heart and give them strength, peace and justice they deserve.

"I ask this in Christ our Savior's Name. Bless you, Lord. Amen."

I wonder how it feels like to pay for a crime you didn't commit.

ॐ∾୬

One of my aunts is so indebted, she has been hiding from everyone.

Message Twenty-Nine

A woman was in debt throughout the entire neighborhood. Day after day, people came to her door asking for their money. She didn't have it. She then addressed a message to God:

"In the Name of the Father, the Son and the Holy Spirit, Amen.

"Jesus Christ of Nazareth, Almighty Father God, Holy Spirit, I've come under your cover. You know the situation I'm presently going through. It isn't my wish to be in such a mess, Oh Father God, but look at me. I have become the wanted one.

"After the death of my capricious husband—may his soul rest in peace—I have taken loan here and there. I borrowed from many people to start a business that didn't work out. Should I believe my hands are tied, that they can't bear fruits? I had hoped to pay each of them off after my business

started to thrive. Unfortunately, I was unable to.
"I'm a fugitive today. They are all after me for their money. They are right, aren't they? But what can I do? I actually don't have any money. I have no intention of stealing. Gracious God, you forbid theft. So I refuse and profess that I'll never steal. Nonetheless, I don't know what to do.*

"Heavenly Father, help me pay back these debts. I wish to pay them back because they were kind-hearted enough to have helped me at a time when I needed them most. But, don't let them harass me anymore. Harassing me makes me crazy. I could become really crazy if they continue.

"Oh Lord, do something for me, please, I beg of you. In your Gracious Name, I pray. Amen."

I remember the day a certain woman caught my aunt. She was furious and wanted her money at all cost. If it hadn't been for the neighbors, she would have killed my aunt.

ॐ∽ॐ

All men are looking for amazingly beautiful women. What about the ugly ones?

Message Thirty

Elisa is an ugly, but well-mannered, twenty-seven year old lady. Naturally, because of her ugliness, men don't want to marry her. This worries her parents. Out of anxiety, Elisa's mother sends a message to God:

"Oh Merciful God, my chest is overloaded and I wish to pour it out. I desire to count my worries to you and put them all in your mighty hands.

Lord, Creator of all nations, you created this world and everything in it. You are the same God who created my daughter and put her in my womb. I didn't refuse nor did I complain. So, don't leave me alone with this burden.

"Before I was twenty, I was already married and pregnant with her. Now, my daughter, Elisa, is twenty-seven and she is unmarried and childless. I don't think it is normal, Lord.

"Now, it is time, God. I call upon you, Jesus Christ, to intervene. Elisa is no longer a child. All her friends, if I may say so, are already married and enjoying their family lives. But my daughter is still single. She needs a man in her life. I pray, Oh Mighty God, you come to her rescue.

"I don't underestimate you, Lord. Please, she's not getting any younger. Intervene now, God. May your Holy Fire burn to ashes all spirits of darkness, and the evil spirits of hindrance.

"Oh Father Lord, take control of the situation my daughter is going through and turn it into victory.

"In Your Holy Name I pray. Amen."

For sure, no matter how ugly she might be, someone will definitely marry her one day.

CHAPTER FOUR

Lord,
give us another chance

Message Thirty-One

I had gone back to the hospital to visit my sick cousin, when I met a man crying and praying in the waiting room.

Due to the complications during delivery, doctors advised the woman and her family that she ought to have surgery. Apart from the huge amount of money involved, the woman's husband was petrified by the news.

He sent a message to God:

"Lord Jesus, she is my wife. My better-half is presently between the devil and the deep sea. She needs you, Lord. I call for your divine intervention, God; the one that free humans from the yoke of evil. This moment is bitter and inevitable. No one can do it but you. We need you, Oh Lord, more than we ever did.

"Forgive us if we've offended you. But, please,

this is the moment. Listen to her outcries, listen, Lord, to our outcries. I know and believe that you can do it because you never change. Help her to deliver safely.

"Oh Eternal Saviour, help the doctors and nurses not to make any mistakes. God of healing, I wish there will be no complication during the caesarean.

Jesus, help us. Bring the baby into this world safely so that he could sing your Name, adore You, and worship You.

"In your Mighty Name, I have pray. Amen.

What a pity. The man was desperate and in need.

അ◌െ◌

Do you have a friend with whom you entrust not only your innermost thoughts, but also your faults as well? If yes, you have to be careful; that person could betray you at any time.

Message Thirty-Two

Rania and Loretta were very good friends. They shared almost everything. But when Rania entered a serious relationship with a guy, Loretta, who didn't have the same opportunity, began to envy her best friend. Ultimately, these friends fell in love with the same guy.

This is Loretta's message to God:

"Oh God, here I am before you. I'm on my knees asking for your infinite forgiveness. I ask forgiveness for my sins, my Lord, either by thoughts or words,

and even those I've committed by my actions or omissions.

"I know you can see straight through me, deep inside my heart, and I can't hide anything from you, my God. I have sinned against my best friend. But, I can't control it. I love her boyfriend.

"Oh Almighty God, Rania doesn't deserve such a wonderful man. Why didn't you give him to me in the first place? He has now taken hold of my heart. I love him so much. I would forsake anything in the world just to have him.

"Meanwhile, Dear God, let them break up. I'm ready to take him. Let them fight and end their relationship so that I can win him over. Let misunderstanding and confusion separate them.

"Oh Heavenly God, he has many things in common with me and not her. I can feel that he loves me too. But, you see, he's in a kind of prison and needs deliverance. Please, Lord, deliver him.

"Oh Jesus Christ, my action may not be good, but try to understand me. I can't help it. I wish to have him, even at my best friend's demise.

"I pray in your Almighty Name. Amen."

How terrible! Such is life, and we should always be aware. Anything can happen.

ත∽ෙ

Dreams could sometimes be very awful.

Message Thirty-Three

A young lady, called Elizabeth, had a nightmare. Frightened, she woke up and started mumbling a message to God:

"Blood of Jesus! Blood of Jesus! Blood of Jesus!

"Oh Lord, you are my shepherd and the mightiest of all warriors. Almighty God, call all your armies to come and fight for me. You are the Creator of heaven and earth. I am your faithful child because I gave my soul to you a long time ago.

"Please, merciful God; I don't know where such an awful dream came from. But wherever it originated, fight it back, Oh God.

"Everything that has just happened in my dream should be harmless and meaningless.

"Yes, I'm a sinner, and you sent your only Son to cleanse and forgive my sins. As a matter of fact, Jesus Christ died for my sins, God.

"Please, Lord, what I saw in my dreams was horrible. God of mercy, you are with me and my soul. Let nothing touches or haunts me. I did no wrong to anyone.

"Oh Misericord God, let your power show on earth. May your burning Fire consume all those who are planning against me. I'm only here to worship and praise you, Oh God.

"In the powerful name of You, God, I pray. Amen."

She was so frightened and scared. Anyway, I guess she will be fine.

ࢳ∘ࢴ

Nowadays, the young people sturggle to get a job. Although some of them have all the qualifications, they usually don't know where to start.

Message Thirty-Four

Anthony is thirty-one years old and jobless. He studied abroad and holds a PhD in International Trade. He sent a message to God:

"In the Name of the Father, the Son and the Holy Spirit, I pray.

"Dear God, I don't exactly know what I've done to you to deserve this. I have dedicated myself to my studies. Yes, it's true that you would never let me down. But why have you refused to listen to my prayer?

"Look! I'm a PhD holder and I still can't find a job. Why? Did I suffer to learn all those years to become hopeless and insignificant? Answer my prayers, Father Lord. Those small jobs you've given me were not my cup of tea. I rejected them in the Name of Jesus. I want to be at the top, Lord. I want to be the boss of all bosses.

"Please, clear the way for me, God, and place me higher. Had I accepted lesser jobs that were given to me, I would have been insulting you. That's why I refused them, God.

"I finished my studies a year ago and still hunting for a job. I want to work in the biggest international institutions. Please God, do it for me.

"Now comes the time to give me the chance to be at the top. Make me whole. After years of suffering, I will never accept to work under other people. Never!

"I pray in your Merciful Name. Amen."

Many Africans generally wait for jobs, while they should actually be looking for ways to create some. My fellow Africans, let us wake up.

∂∾ᖶ

I don't know about you, but I always dream
of having twins. Yeah, it's true.

Message Thirty-Five

Coffi and Codjo are twins. Coffi got the chance to
travel abroad, while Codjo was left behind. After some
years, Coffi sent seventy-five percent of his savings to
his twin brother to buy a land, and build a big, beautiful house for the family. Codjo received the money, and
built the house in his own name. Later on, he would
ask for God's hand:

*"Thank you, Lord. This is the time I can really
confirm that you truly love all of us. You love us the
same and equal way. We praise your noble heart.*

*"You gave my twin brother the chance to go
overseas and make money. And he did. I'm sure
you were thinking that he would help me once he
got there. Well, he didn't. Now that he'd sent me
money to build the family house, I'm certain that
I'm not part of his plan. He just wants to use me.
I can feel it.*

*"Therefore, not to be stupid, the entire project
now belongs to me. I ought to take advantage of him
before I regret.*

*"Please, don't condemn me, Lord. Try to understand my concerns. This is the only way I can ensure
my future, and the future of my four children. I
know he has made so much money that taking this
out of it wouldn't be a problem.*

*"Please Lord, I need a favor. Help me play tricks
on him. Keep my twin brother abroad. I don't want
him coming back home to cause any trouble. Let him
die there and never think of coming home.*

"Almighty God, let my brother never talk about this money again. He should completely forget he gave it to me for building the family house. It is now my personal property, the home for my wife and children alone. Do it for me, God. This is all I'm asking you this morning.

"I pray in the Name of the Father, the Son and the Holy Spirit. Amen."

I am speechless up to this point. If you have something to say, you're welcome to say it.

ॐ✦

Some pastors behave in a way that God despises. Anyway, human beings should be very attentive and observant, for we have many wolves disguised in sheep's clothing nowadays.

For a better understanding, read '**War of Morality**' by Augustine Sherman. Why? Because, there is a terrible conflict going on between man and the church.

Message Thirty-Six

After entering his church in the morning, a pastor sent this message to God:

"Baba God, I'm nothing without you. You are the one who ordered me to wake up and I did. If you had said, 'No,' I wouldn't have woken. I give you praise.

"Today is another day, King of Kings. My doors are opened. Help me, God, to have a lot of clients. Create confusion in their lives and send them straight to me for solutions. As you did miracles through your Beloved Son, help me be a star. Let the entire world talk about me. Let me be a testimony.

"You know how stubborn human beings are. They never learn if there is no hardship or problem. Therefore, I wish they get themselves into trouble, difficulties and problems that they cannot solve any on their own.

"I pray this morning they discover the bitter side of the world and run for shelter. Oh Lord, help me with miracles, because they will never believe if they don't see. They are all just like Thomas.

"Merciful God, I wish they get caught in the twining net of Satan and his folks, so that through me, they can find solutions. Like that, let them run to my temple, Your temple for a hideout.

"Eternal God, I hope I'm not asking too much. In case if I am, forgive me. I'm just worried about your kingdom that's all. Help me to do this work you sent me for.

"In the Name of the Almighty, I pray. Amen."

Is that 'Man of God' really worried about the kingdom of God? Or his own kingdom? Such a message coming from a man of God… frankly, I can't imagine.

ॐॐ

Men are ready to do anything at will to be wealthy; even if it includes killing.

Message Thirty-Seven

Once upon a time, Mr. Francis was a very poor guy. He was worth nothing, and everybody laughed at him.

Finally, in order to become wealthy, he sacrificed his only child to an evil sect. In fact, all the sect members were also rich.

Mr. Francis sent a message to God:

"Oh God, I recognize what I've gotten myself into is totally wrong and evil. I know that you are the Almighty. But, you didn't leave me any choice.

"I was suffering as if I was the one who killed your Son, Jesus Christ. Because of my hardship, I ended up making a wicked decision. I know I sacrificed my only son, just like you sacrificed Jesus for the humanity. I'm not comparing myself to you, but I'm only following your steps.

"Forgive me, Lord, but your way is too long and slow. As human beings, we can't always wait that long... not all of us. I lost my patience and this is where it has led me. My innocent child was sacrificed. He paid the price for me to be rich. Please, welcome him in your kingdom.

"Now, I'm very rich and respected by all. The same people that were laughing at me are now begging me. This world is such a miracle. Oh Misericord God, I know that I won't get away with this. There is a price to pay. And yes, I'll gladly pay for it. But at least, I won't suffer in this world anymore.

"Furthermore, I'm making my family and children very rich. I'm praying to you, High God, may you lessen my pains and help me go through this.

"When the time comes, I mean judgment day, don't ask me too many questions, because you already know everything. The group I have joined

said that I'm no longer yours. But in my heart, I'm with you... I am yours.

"High God, Creator of heaven and earth, I'm strongly with you. Even if I deny you before them, you know my heart. Please, rescue me if there is still a chance. But remember, I don't want to lose my wealth.

"Please keep me blessed with this abundance of wealth. I wish you received my message.

"To You, High God I pray. Amen."

May the Lord listen to his message, if it is worthy.

ॐॐ

I read a book one day and discovered something; a little eight-year-old boy faced God with a question.

Message Thirty-Eight

Mathias is a little eight-year-old boy. He knelt beside his bed and sent a message to God with a pertinent question:

"… Amen.

"God, invisible God, I hope you are fine today. They say Jesus Christ is your Son. They also say that you are the Creator of heaven and earth; you created everything on the ground and underground. You must be very powerful to do that—that's what they say, Almighty God.

"I have heard that you love all of us, and that you never wish anything bad to happen to us. That is so kind of you. But since I was born, I see humas cry everyday. I wonder why.

"I've seen the sufferings of humans in the papers, watched it on TV and everywhere I go. Children are crying, soldiers are dying, and women are always in pain. War is everywhere, and many people are homeless. Some people are helpless and others are just unlucky.

"Why have you abandoned us? Why should you abandon the world? Many people are dying and you don't do anything about it. When someone dies, their family members cry a lot. They say, 'God has given, God has taken.'

"I don't understand. Don't you have a wife and kids? How big is your house to carry all these people you are taking? You have my grandparents, and I've missed my granddaddy so much.

"Please, God, if you don't mind, it hurts when you take them away. Don't get angry, but I don't want you to take my parents. I love them and they love me too. We are a happy family.

"Thank you for listening to me, God. Amen."

Admirable, isn't it? Kids are so smart and intelligent nowadays. But, there are many things they are yet to understand.

෨ඏ

The New Year has come, and everyone is sending a message to God.

Message Thirty-Nine

Last year was long and hectic. Now it's the New Year, and everyone has wishes. A young man faces God with the following message concerning the New Year:

"Once again, I thank you, God, for my life and for bringing me through last year. You are the Alpha and Omega. You make all things possible according to your will.

"For me personally, last year was hard and difficult; though you guided me through. I have come here to give thanks for all you have done for me throughout the years. I want to say thank you for protecting me and watching over me all along.

"Many people have found death along the way, but you kept me alive. Many persons encountered several problems last year, and fell on the way. Powers of darkness have struck many, while leaving others with false hopes and expectations. Yes, the year wasn't perfect for me; yet, I'm not counted among the dead. And for that I thank you, God.

"Heavenly father, I pray that this year will be my best year. I pray for the past to be gone and buried. If I survived the difficult past until this New Year, I guess I must be a winner. If that's the case, I believe the Lord has obviously made me a winner for a reason... for a straight purpose.

"Almighty God, help me find my destiny. I wish this New Year would be fruitful and peaceful. I bless the Lord to give me strength and life, to be able to do great things in the world.

"Oh Lord, may every sickness, weakness and sorrow be lifted far away from me and my household. I pray that You, Lord, fight every principalities and evil spirits that intend to attack me, or go after my life; my life belongs to You alone.

"I pray, Jesus of Nazareth, to be my witness, and with his wisdom, help me understand answers to different preoccupations. This New Year is in the name of the Almighty God, the beginning of a new

world and the future of a new generation.
"I pray in the Powerful Name of Jesus Christ
of Nazareth. Amen."

By the way, may this coming year be a blessing to everyone.

ॐ∽ॐ

When a young person gets sick, we are scared and we pray. What if an elderly person, almost a hundred years of age, gets a heart attack?

Message Forty

A ninety-nine-year-old woman had a heart attack. The children quickly took her to the hospital where she was saved. While she was on the hospital bed receiving treatment, her eldest daughter send a message to God:

"Please, Heavenly God, do something about this case. My mother is very sick and I have no strength to save her but you. No doctor could do anything without you, Lord. Oh Father, listen to my prayer and my cries.

"Father God, I don't want my mother to die at this age. Let her live a little longer, my God. Please God, come to her rescue.

"Right now, I don't even have the cash to bury her. I know my brothers have the means, but I don't. At least, let me save enough so they wouldn't laugh at me at the burial.

"Do you see why you need to spare her life? Heavenly God, I plead you do this for me.

"In the Name of the One who created heaven

and earth, I pray. Amen."

So at any age, as humans, we are really never ready to see our parents die. Should they live eternally? Or tell me, at what age will a man accept or be happy to see his parents die without any complain?

CHAPTER FIVE

May you,
God, dwell in our hearts

My uncle prays for the new season always.

Message Forty-One

A farmer plowed his land to prepare for the coming season, and sent a message to God.

"I'm ready at last, Dear God. You've helped me prepare everything to welcome the next season; as it is fast approaching, I'm ready now to sow. I only hope you stay with me right through until the next harvest. I'm sowing tomatoes, peppers and onions.

Heavenly Father, let this new season be the most amazing. Up to now, I know my previous works have been quite impressive with very good results.

"Please, Lord, may the rain fall and the sun shine, always at the appropriate time. I've spent all my resources and money this season, God, and I expect to reap it in tenfold. In the end, let me laugh

with pride and glorify your Name.
"Yes, Father God, I call upon you to secure my
field and make my efforts meaningful. Please, Lord,
help my cultivation to be the best ever. Oh Christ,
all I'm asking for is the gain after my hard work.
"In your Almighty Name I pray. Amen."

So I wouldn't have to buy tomatoes, pepper and
onions, may the Lord hear your prayer, dear uncle.

ॐॐ

Once they are in the delivering room, pregnant women become crazy. They say all
sorts of things.

Message Forty-Two

A pregnant woman, practically on the verge of
giving birth, raised her voice and talked directly to
God:

"Praise the Lord! Alleluia.
"My God, my Savior; I've come to give myself
to you. Jesus Christ, my shepherd, I've come filled
with hope that you will stand by me. I know you've
done it for many women, but this is my first time...
my first delivery... my first fear. However, knowing
you are with me, Lord, I will fear nothing.
"Dear God, the baby may come any minute
now and I'm counting on you. Assist me, uphold
me, and cover me with the Blood of Jesus Christ
your only Son.
"It is a crucial moment for any woman going
through this experience. I imagine it's long and
excruciating. But with you, my God at the wheel,

I feel safer.

"Help me, Lord, to deliver without any compli-cation. My greatest fear is called, surgery. I reject any idea leading to that end.

"Oh Father Protector, let my child come into this world safely. Let him be healthy and sound. I know with you, all things are possible. That is why I have come to you.

"Lord, once again, show me you are the only one. When all is said and done, I will shout your Name with joy.

"This is my message in your Holy Name. Amen."

One of my aunts used to say, "God will always watch over his owns. Therefore, we shouldn't fear."

ॐ∞ॐ

I wish to have four children. Having just one isn't bad, but having more is better.

Message Forty-Three

Kotey and Grace are married with one son. He is almost twelve years old. They are not fortunate to have another child. One day, the boy woke up in the middle of the night, knelt down by his bed and sent God a message:

"My Father God, right now, I know you can see and hear me. Please, I have a big problem I wish you could help me solve. Only you can help me find a solution to it. I am twelve years old now. My parents have not been able to get another child, and it worries me a lot. I can see on their faces that it

worries them too. I don't really know why they are having this problem, but I bet you know. So, please God, bless them with another child.

"I feel lonely. I have neither a brother nor a sister to play with. When I look around, I see other kids laughing, walking down the street hand in hand with their siblings. I can only imagine how wonderful it must be. I long to have siblings of my own too. So, God, please, I need a brother or a sister.

"When I go to school, or to the library, the church, or even on the streets, I see brothers and sisters. They are always together while I'm always alone. Please, Lord, I wish you listen to my prayer and answer me.

"I pray to you, God, in the Name of your Son, Christ. Amen."

Unity is strength. Being alone is nothing compared to loneliness or boredom. Gracious God, help that kid.

ੋੋਓ

I have a friend called, Danny. He might be physically handicapped, but he is very intelligent and wise. God should help people like him.

Message Forty-Four

A handicapped man cried out to God every single day. He said all kinds of things that might bring him favor. He sent God his messages like this:

"God Almighty, Creator of the universe, I praise YOU. I lift your name and look to you. Oh Father God, wherever you are, please listen to my call. I

need you in my life.

"Jesus Christ of Nazareth, as usual, I have come to ask for your mercy. I will never get tired until you bless my petition, Oh Lord. You created me like this, and I am sure I don't look like the others. I'm far different from them. I always ask you why, God.

"I know for everything there is a reason. My incapacity prevents me from a lot of things ordinary people do with ease. My handicap is worse than the most common man. I know for you it is normal, but for a human it isn't. People sometimes laugh at me and mock me. I hear them giggling. What can I do other than call out your Name?

"Dear God, I know you have a specific plan for my life. Please show me the way. Holy Spirit, I need guidance and protection.

"Father Lord, clear my mind and set for me a wonderful goal. Let humanity be astonished to see Thy power.

"My God, I pray for your mercy and wisdom. Save me from humiliation. I'm nobody without you, and I know you will never abandon me. With this said, I wish you to answer my message before it is too late.

"In your Powerful Name I pray. Amen."

By now, I believe he must have found a way. In fact, it's been a long time since I heard from him.

കരുക

We already know doctors need God's blessing while attending patients, or when in surgery. But what if people are healthy?

Message Forty-Five

For the last ten years, Doctor James Hospital has been one of the best in town. Doctor James is always in communication with God. He send this message to God:

"Thank you, Lord. You are indeed my God. First, I suffered; then you rewarded me. I am grateful for all wonders in my life. You are the only doer, and I'm convinced you will keep on doing for me.

"This hospital has saved the lives of many people in this country. It has cured an immeasurable number of people from all over this country. This is because, Heavenly Father, you stand by our side while we are working night and day. I've come to realized, life is a dream. You perceive it the way you dreamt it.

"Now that we are the number one hospital in the country, help me to not fall again. We are the head, let us shall never become the tail.

"Father God, I have one more favor to ask. Please don't misunderstand me. The more people get sick, suffer from ailments, or contagious and deadly diseases, the better the hospital works, sells, and builds its reputation. So, never stop allowing humans to contract diseases such as AIDS, malaria, cholera, cancer, and most recently, Ebola. I'm happy when I hear such news because I know my hospital will welcome many victims; which means money. If it continues like this, I'll become a billionaire in the next twenty years.

"Ebola has affected numerous victims so far, and I benefited from it. Jehovah, my Father, I can't do this alone. Protect all the staff from the diseases they are curing.

"I pray in the Name of Almighty God. Amen."

How come a human being, like you and I, could be so wicked? Perhaps, he thinks he's helping the world. What I really don't understand is, his prayer is for us to get sick. How doughty!

సౌ

Incidentally, I heard the message of a young man who lost his wife in a car accident.

Message Forty-Six

A young married man lost his wife in a car accident. On hearing of her death, he cried profusely, but unfortunately, it couldn't bring back his beloved. The least he could do was to pray for her innocent soul. He sent this message to God:

"Oh, why, my God? I assume you know the reason because there is nothing that you don't know. I bless you for that. But as you can see, I'm a mere mortal. Please, Lord, don't blame me for my attitude right now. She was all I had; she was my sister, mother, aunt, counselor... my everything.

"Apart from you, God, there was nothing I wanted or needed that I didn't see or have in her. Now that she's gone, I don't know what I'm going to become.

"It is like I have no more reason to live, but rest assured that I have no desire to hasten my demise. You see, Lord, right now, I'm in a kind of dilemma.

"Oh Father God, don't abandon me. I need you now more than ever. Sure, I imagine there must be a reason for my suffering. Therefore, I'll try to stay strong and healthy for my only child. I know very

well he needs me.

"God, please bless and protect him. I know that there is no better protector than you. Help me to take good care of him. As for my dear wife, she will always remain in my heart, like a tattoo on my skin. Please Lord, welcome her in your noble kingdom. God of mercy, make sure that her soul rests in perfect peace.

"In the Almighty Name I pray. Amen."

That's life for us; we must accept the unexpected.

∽◦⌒

Men say women are not trustworthy. Women shout men are like goats. Who do you believe?

Message Forty-Seven

Karl and Fatou got married legally. They were very happy until one day Karl met Bernice. His love and attitude towards Fatou began to change. Now, Karl is no longer in love with Fatou, he loves Bernice instead. He sent this message to God:

"Father Lord, I sincerely regret to have married Fatou. Today, I have come to realize that she is not my better half. God, you know my heart. You know I didn't plan to hurt Fatou. Now, this is the situation.

"To be honest, she didn't do me any wrong. I just don't love her anymore. Since I met Bernice, I realized my mistake. I know Bernice is the one my heart beats for. I can even feel that with Bernice, my heart beats faster. Oh Jesus Christ, help me through this mess.

"All I want is to make things easier for both of us. I don't wish to torment Fatou. Therefore, I'm asking for a divorce. I prefer to marry Bernice. So, help me to convince Fatou about this. Please, let me get my divorce from her easily. I plead in the Name of your only Son, Christ.

"And so shall it be. I pray in Thy Almighty Name. Amen."

Today we're in love; tomorrow we think it wasn't love. After satisfying our lust, we change, redirecting our sights to a new adventure. May God bless this world.

ॐॐ

Guess what? Many sacrileges are being committed today.

Message Forty-Eight

Based on the situation he is going through in his own home, a father sends a message to God. This is the message:

"Oh God of mercy, have mercy on me. Your words declare that we sin in many ways. Even by thought, we have already sinned. I have come to you to forgive me.

"My first daughter will turn twenty-five years old soon, and her presence in the house is driving me crazy. Forgive me, Lord, but, I've decided to confess it; especially the way she dresses—almost naked.

"Nowadays, you know how ladies in the world have changed—television, fashion, where all the girls want to be at the cutting edge. Whenever I look

at her chest and butt, my mind gets hot and I start sweating. Please Lord, make sure she gets a husband and leave my compound before I commit a sacrilege.

"God of mercy, I'll accept any man that brings her dowry; and of course, that she wants to be with.

"Please, do it for me before it is too late. It's not that I'm in love with my own daughter, but her waist, her mouth… her breasts are so provoking that I don't know if I can control myself. Forgive me, Lord; she is so appealing and challenging. I want her out of my house, but I can't dismiss her. She hasn't done anything bad to me, God.

"How am I going to cope with this? Please, Lord, I need your help. Bless her and let her get a good husband, someone who would take good care of her. Please, God of mercy, have mercy on me.

"I pray in your Merciful Name. Amen."

Can you believe it? It's true. Tell me, could you feel that way about your own daughter? Abomination!

ॐ✌

A friend of mine confessed to me that she
saw someone being raped.

Message Forty-Nine

A young lady was an eyewitness to a rape incident. She saw everything, but she was frightened to death of saying a word. They would no doubt kill her, she reasoned. So, when she was called to the witness stand, she lied. Later, she cried and sent a message to God:

"Please, God, forgive me. You know I'm an eyewitness to what happened. But I dared not say

a word. My God, what have I done? I denied every single thing at the bar.

"Oh Lord of mercy, please don't be hard on me. They would kill me if I say a word. I don't think the police can protect me either, Lord. I'm very afraid. I'm afraid of everything now.

"Where am I going to hide? I feel like running far away from human wickedness. Forgive me, Lord, for not being strong enough to face this case.

"My regret now is that those criminals will get away with their crime, owing to the fact there is no evidence against them. I'm really sorry for the woman that was sexually abused. I'm sorry I couldn't help her. But, I know Dear God, you can help expose those criminals. I pray to you, Oh Lord, don't let them get away with it. Above all, please forgive me, God.

"I pray in your Powerful Name. Amen."

I do understand why the lady did what she did. She was afraid and under pressure not to say a word. What would you have done?

ॐ∽ॐ
This guy had never pray before. Now he needs God.

Message Fifty

A certain man never believed in God. But, like most of us when everything falls apart, God turns out to be our last hope. That is exactly what happened to this man. And so, he sends a message to God:

"God... I've never pray before. I don't know

what to say. I don't even know where to start. I am so sorry, please forgive me. All I know is I need you, and... I believe. Just show me what to do. Amen!"

God is kind; He listens to everyone.

APPENDIX

If you've read these messages well, I am certain you were surprised at many of their substances. You may have wondered and desired to understand why some people pray the way they do. But they do, and their desires, however seemingly unorthodox, go to the essence of God's wisdom in creating each of us the way He did.

While some of these prayers were rather funny, even silly at times, others were serious and most touching. The bottom line is, they all carry intent to achieve pacifications or solutions to situations and problems affecting individual lives.

We all attempt to reach or connect with God in different ways. The contexts of those variations reflect the level of not only our individual understanding of God, but our particular relationship we believe we share with Him. Day after day, night after night, every minute we ask, we beg and pray, not just in hope, but with the conviction that God will eventually do it for us.

Still, where do our messages go? Which direction do they often take? When we send our prayers, demands or grievances in a good or bad way, how does God take them?

Each, I suspect, goes to God's understanding and

knowledge of what He believes is best for us. Nonetheless, I imagine how God feels about us is evident in the fact that He has given us the ability to choose right from wrong. While through these choices we may err, feel disappointments, suffer physical and emotional pain, it is by these trials and errors are true understanding and knowledge achieved.

Because God is all understanding, all knowledge and all wisdom, coming in oneness with Him require His children to obtain characteristics similar to His.

This then justifies why God gave us freedom of choice by which trials and errors are effected. If considered as such, we can understand how a father feels when a child approaches him under these circumstances.

CONNECT WITH AUTHOR

Readers of this book are encouraged to contact
Mr. Houngnikpo with comments:
E-mail: oliverkann100@yahoo.fr

Visit author's Facebook Page
www.facebook/houngnipko.frankolivier.com

Get updates on upcoming books at:
www.villagetalespublishing.houngnipko.com

Other Books by Village Tales Publishing

By Ophelia S. Lewis
Dead Gods HM2
Heart Men (A Novel)
Montserrado Stories
Good Manner Alphabets
My Dear Liberia (Recollections)
Journeys (a Collection of Poems)
The Dowry of Virgins (and Other Stories)

By Augustine B. Sherman
War of Morality

By Franck Olivier Houngnikpo
Message To God

AVAILABLE WHEREVER BOOKS ARE SOLD.

Coming Soon!
By Shedrick B. Seton
The Falcon

By Ophelia S. Lewis
Liberia UnScrabbled

೭∞೯

All Village Tales Publishing titles, imprints and distributed lines are available at special quantity discounts for bulk purchased for sales promotions, premiums, fundraising, educational or institutional use.

For information, please Visit our website
www.villagetalespublishing.com

Join our mailing list and get updates on new releases, deals, bonus content and other great books from Village Tales Publishing.

Email:
villagetalespub@gmail.com
info@villagetalespublishing.com

Like Us on Facebook
www.facebook.com/villagetalespublishing

૭ન્

Village Tales Publishing provides traditional publishing services and turnkey services to individuals that seek to successfully self-publish and promote their books. We handle all aspects of publishing—editing, cover design, production, marketing and order fulfillment.

Please visit our websites:
www.villagetalespublishing.com
www.oass.villagetalespublishing.com